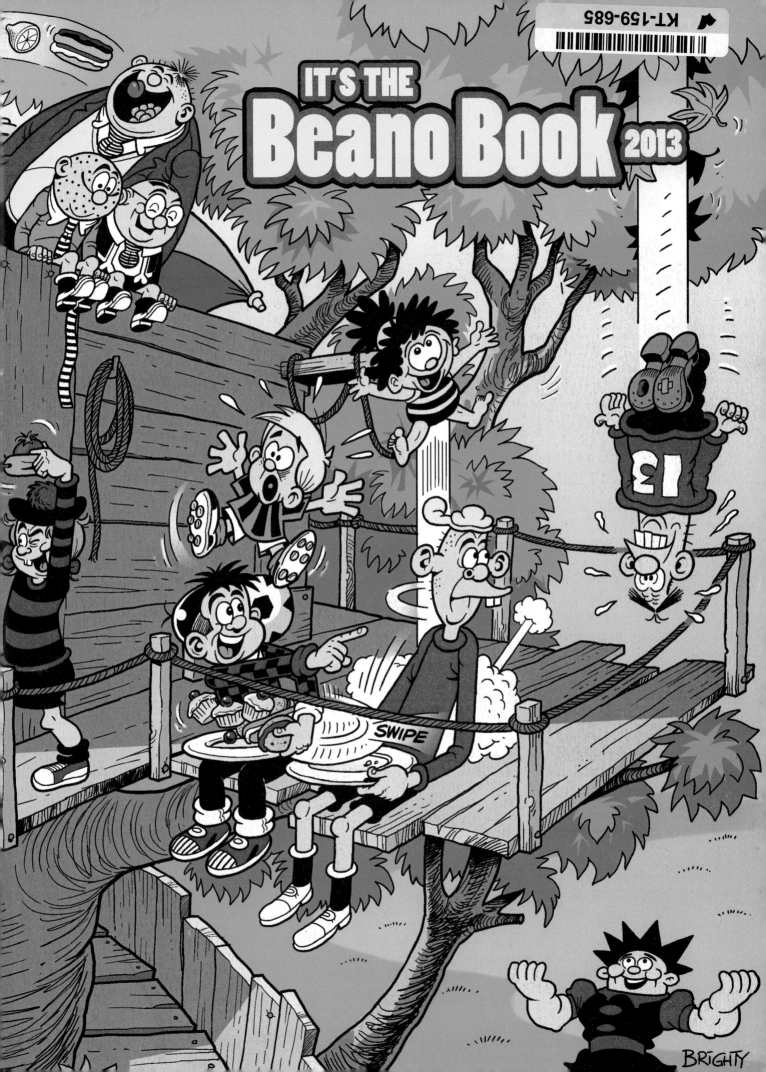

IT'S THE Beano Book 2013

THE BEANO

1938 — 2013

75 ·YEARS OF LAUGHTER!·

THIS BOOK BELONGS TO:

Eilidh Campbell

Eubhal

Kilmore

This is really cool! You have loads of fun and nobody can see you.

Yeah.

NEXT DAY... Your Dad was well cool yesterday.

Yeah. He's...

...he's... here?

Hiya, Dennis. I invited some of my pals to the tree-house to skive... I mean... chill out.

My Fifth medal...

Blah-blah...

They've invaded our tree-house. This is really rubbish!

Tax returns...

Politics...

Boring guff...

NEXT DAY...

Come on, lads. We can hide out in the tree-house again.

Nine-nil down... and it's only half-time!

Ah... but we'll be shooting downhill second half, guys. We can still win!

It's no good – we'll never score ten to get to the cup final!

NO ENTRY

I need something to gee them up – I'll need this!

DAVE EASTBURY

Do you know what this is? This is Mr Ned. A lucky mascot owned by my Grandad. Fourteen hours down t'pit he used to work and then play football.

PONG!

A very old, very smelly, fluffy donkey? Poo-ee!

But I'll tell you this... this mascot helped his team – Jarrow Colliery FC – win the cup! And now it'll help you too!

Jarrow Colliery? Who are they?

Exactly, mate!

Jose Mourinho couldn't have done that better! Ho-ho!

GGRRRRRR!

CUP FINAL

PIE SHOP

Crumbs! How will I Find Mr Ned in this crowd?

WHY DON'T YOU SEE IF YOU CAN FIND MR NED? SEE IF COACH CAN FIND THE LUCKY MASCOT BEFORE THE FINAL BEGINS ON PAGE 100! BEANO ED.

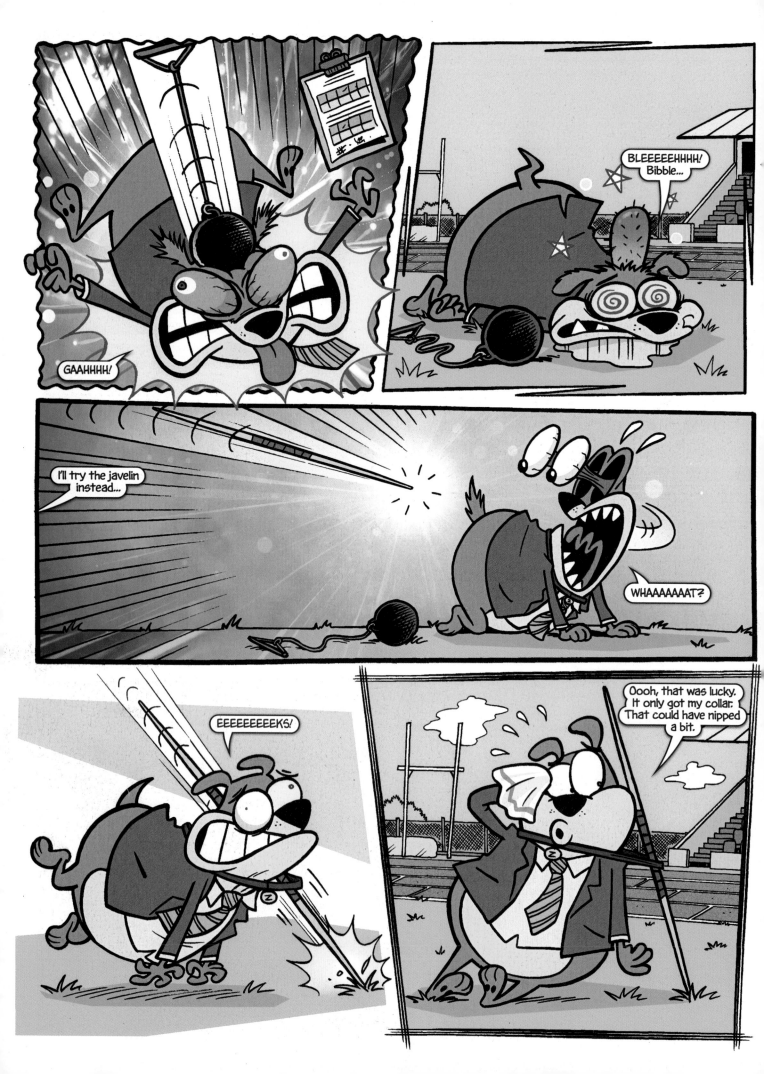

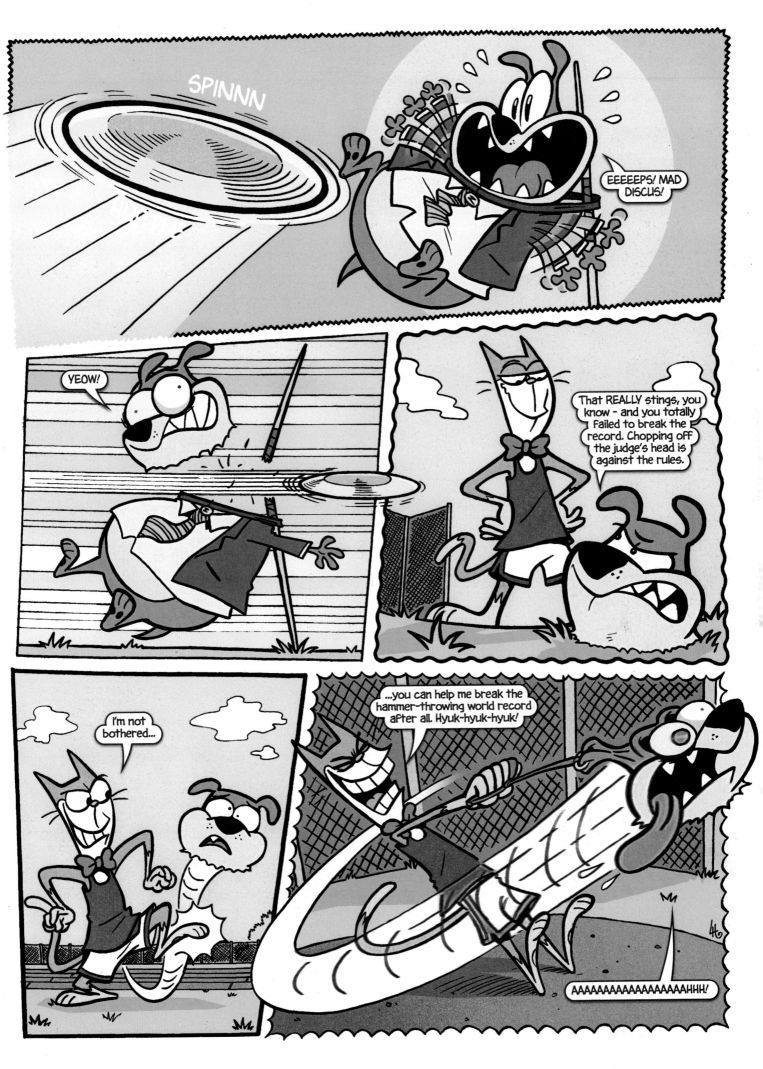

Barry Glennard

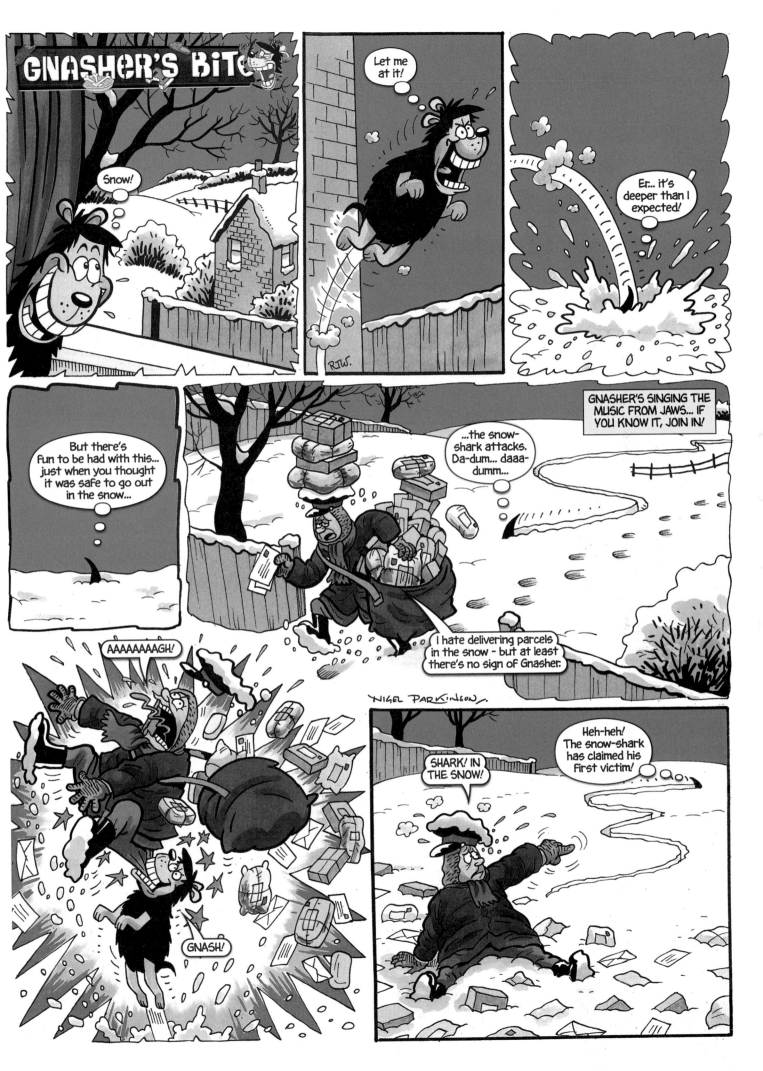

THE BASH STREET KIDS

Bash Street's not much of a tourist destination...

Lovely! BREATHE DEEPLY!

Here comes the tourist bus! Must be to see the beauty spot.

BRMM!

CHIRP! TWEET!

... but it does have a beauty spot!

Let's wave to the nice people!

BRRM

MEEBO & ZUKY's History of VIOLENCE

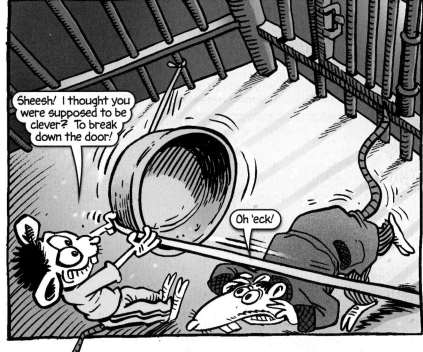

DRAMA CLASS—

Today, children, we will be rehearsing the Scottish play!

The Scottish play? It says 'Macbeth' here!

MACBETH By Some Guy

Wingle, wangle, save this show from a tangle!

Huh? What are you doing?

The Scottish play is cursed! Should you say the title out loud, you must spin three times and use the rhyme I just did to rid the bad luck!

Bad luck, eh? Just 'cos I said 'Macbeth'?

Wingle, wangle, save this show from a tangle!

Ho-ho!

Macb—

No you don't. And you can say 'goodbye' to a part too!

Harrumph! Grumpy, ol' teacher. I'm off to find someone who will appreciate my actin'!

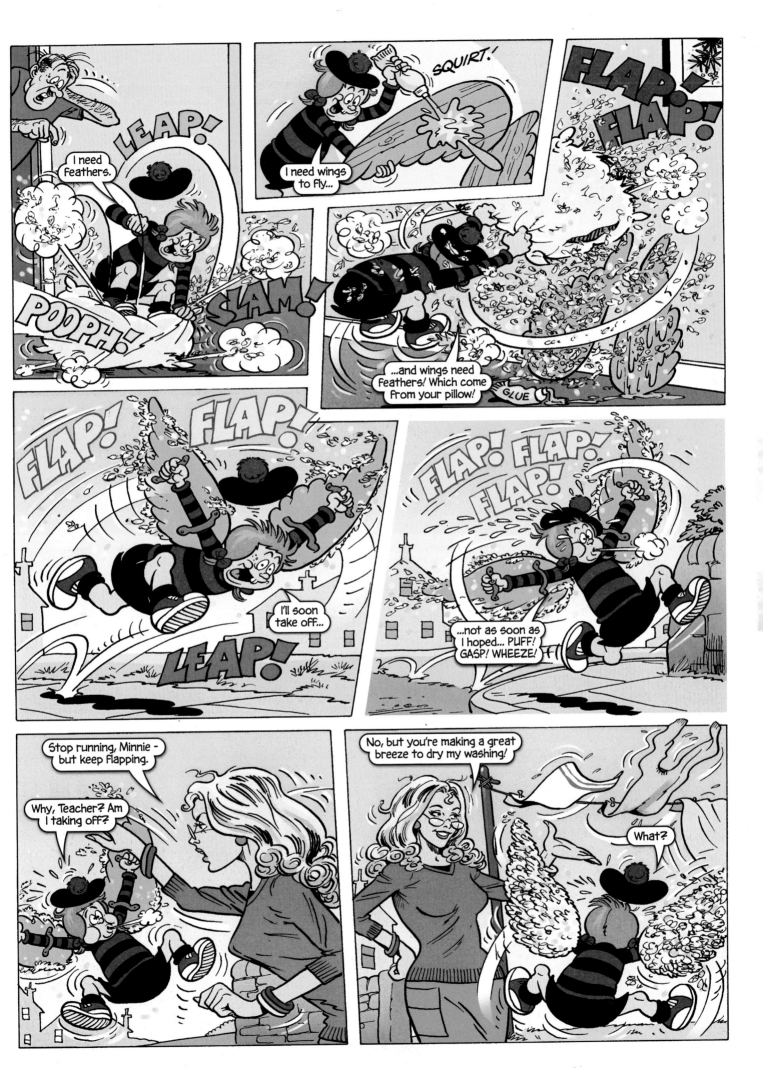

48 seconds!

It's official - I can cook faster than a microwave oven!

EEPS!

THUD! THUD! THUD!

Yikes!

WHUMF!

BANANAMAN! IN THE BIG CHILL

Even the phone sounds cold.

BRRRRRR!

'Tis Chief O'Reilly.

Oh really?

NO, O'REILLY! GET BANANAMAN HERE NOW!

If he needs Bananaman, I need a banana...

...except all my bananas have frozen solid!

TAP! TAP!

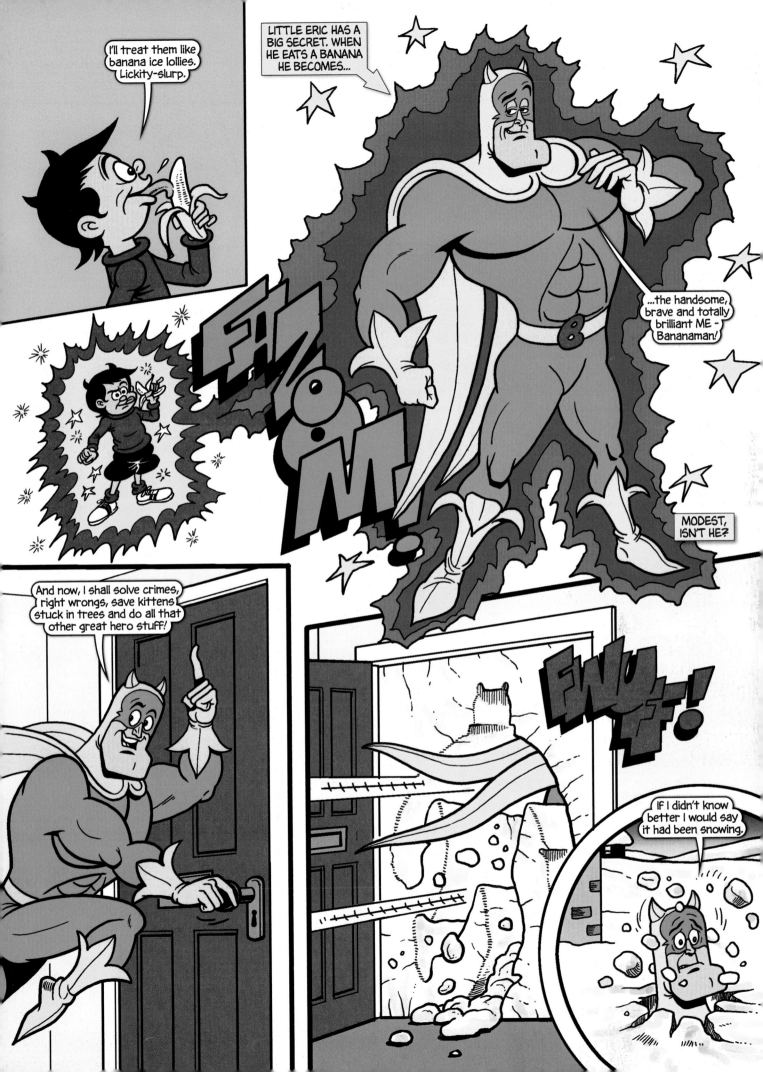

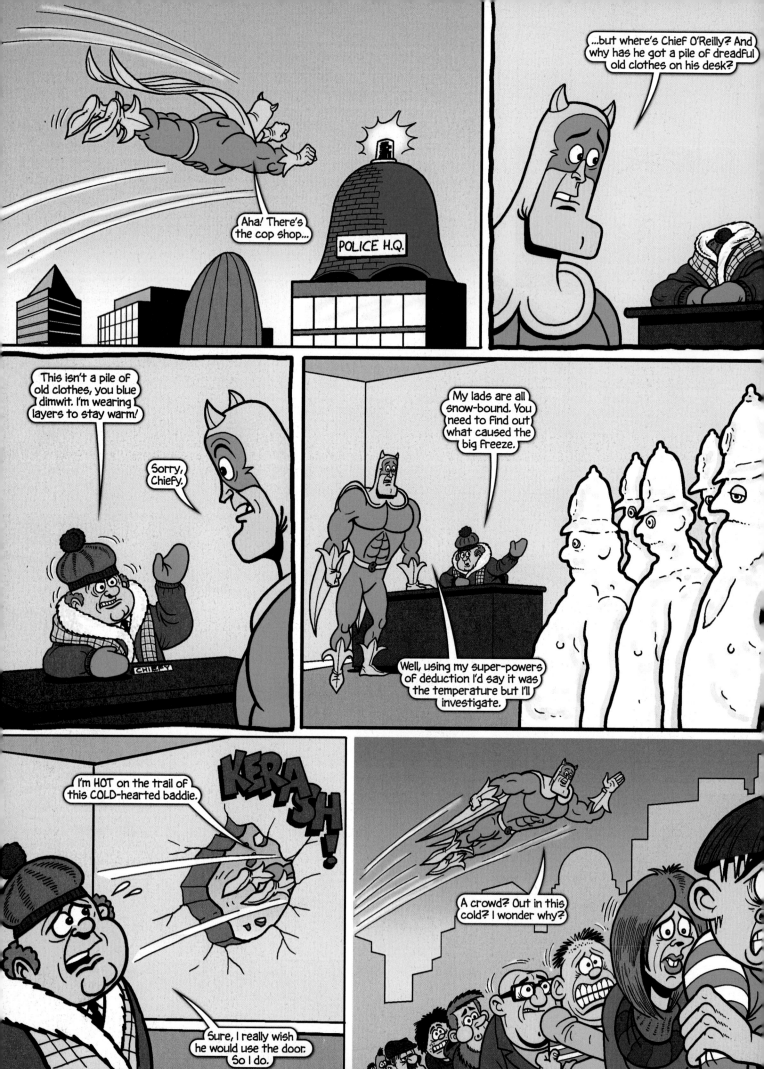

Morning, Roger. I've got a joke for you. What's a mower for?

I don't know, Dad. What's a mower for?

Gardening, Roger! Ha-ha! You'll need these too!

Harrumph! Rotten Dad-joke. Walked right into that one, didn't I?

And this garden's really overgrown! It's going to take more effort than I like to put in... like any at all! I need a dodge!

SO –

Explain this to me again...

I told you – it's simple...

...we sign up to a sports club.

Which one?

SIGN ON!
HOCKEY
AMERICAN
FOOTBALL
CRICKET
BASEBALL

BEANOTOWN SPORTS CLUB

All of them!

Right. What now?

GNASH!

GNASH!

GNASH!

YEOW!

ARGH!

I'm suddenly glad we got all that padded sports' gear.

It was worth a gnashing to get this! A bone's just what I need!

BACK IN DENNIS' GARDEN –

?

Gnuh?

The next stage of my dodge comes here!

Huh?

BEANOTOWN ARCHAEOLOGICAL SOCIETY

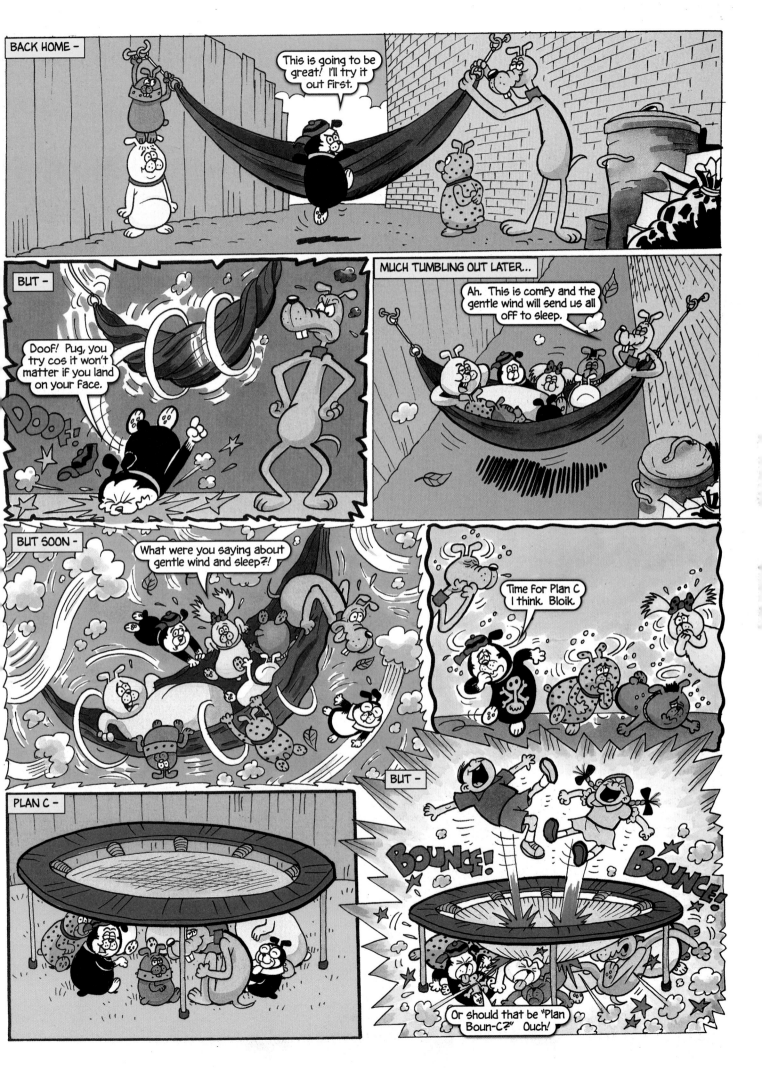

BONKERS BIRTHDAY OFFER FOR THE BEANO FANS!

15 ISSUES

FOR ONLY £15

GR8 REASONS TO SIGN UP!

- Never miss an issue of your favourite comic.
- Get your copy sent to you before it's in the shops!
- Special subscriber offers!
- Get the latest laughs, jokes and pranks before anyone else!
- Includes all cover promotions! Post free delivery.
- Save on the shop price.

WHAT TO DO...

Ask a parent or guardian to help.

Visit: **www.Beano.com/BNAN2**

Call **0800 318 846** 8am-9pm, 7 days.

When ordering please quote code BNAN2

UNDISPUTED
IT'S THE CHEAPEST AND FASTEST WAY TO GET BRITAIN'S FAVOURITE COMIC!

2013 BEANO SURVEY

£200 IN CASH PRIZES TO BE WON!

OUR CUSTOMERS AND READERS ARE IMPORTANT TO US AND YOUR OPINIONS REALLY MATTER. WE WANT THE BEANO ANNUAL TO PROVIDE THE PERFECT READ AND EXPERIENCE, SO PLEASE TAKE THE TIME TO FILL IN THIS SURVEY TO LET US KNOW IF WE ARE GETTING THIS RIGHT.

FILLING IN OUR QUESTIONNAIRE IS EASY

IT'S FASTER AND EASIER TO GO TO

WWW.COMPLETEASURVEY.CO.UK/BEANOANNUAL2013

ALTERNATIVELY COMPLETE THE PAPER COPY AND POST TO: 2013 BEANO ANNUAL SURVEY FREEPOST RSKR-YGJG-XERH CONSUMER INSIGHT DEPARTMENT 80 KINGSWAY EAST DUNDEE DD4 8SL (NO STAMP IS REQUIRED) IF YOU ARE UNDER 16 PLEASE ASK AN ADULT'S PERMISSION BEFORE COMPLETING THE SURVEY. ALL ONLINE AND POSTAL SURVEYS RETURNED BY 1ST MARCH 2013 WILL BE ENTERED INTO A DRAW TO WIN A TOP PRIZE OF £100 AND 2 PRIZES OF £50!

IF YOU WOULD LIKE TO BE ENTERED INTO THE PRIZE DRAW, PLEASE FILL IN YOUR DETAILS BELOW (OPTIONAL)

TITLE .... FIRST NAME .... LAST NAME ....

ADDRESS ....

....

....

POSTCODE .... EMAIL ADDRESS ....

YOUR REPLIES TO THIS QUESTIONNAIRE WILL BE TREATED WITH THE STRICTEST CONFIDENCE AND USED FOR STATISTICAL PURPOSES ONLY. HOWEVER, FROM TIME TO TIME THE PUBLISHERS OF THIS ANNUAL, DC THOMSON & CO LTD AND CAREFULLY SELECTED THIRD PARTIES MAY WISH TO CONTACT YOU VIA POST OR EMAIL WITH OFFERS AND PROMOTIONS. IF YOU WOULD PREFER NOT TO BE CONTACTED PLEASE TICK THE RELEVANT BOX(ES).

☐ I DO NOT WANT TO BE CONTACTED BY THE PUBLISHER OF THIS ANNUAL, DC THOMSON & CO LTD.

☐ I DO NOT WANT TO BE CONTACTED BY THIRD PARTIES.

DID YOU BUY THE BEANO ANNUAL OR RECEIVE IT AS GIFT FROM SOMEONE?

☐ I BOUGHT IT
☑ I RECEIVED IT AS A GIFT (PLEASE PROCEED TO SECTION B)

A PLEASE ONLY ANSWER THE FOLLOWING QUESTIONS IF YOU BOUGHT THIS ANNUAL

IN WHICH MONTH DID YOU PURCHASE THE BEANO ANNUAL?

☐ JANUARY   ☐ FEBRUARY   ☐ MARCH
☐ APRIL   ☐ MAY   ☐ JUNE
☐ JULY   ☐ AUGUST   ☐ SEPTEMBER
☐ OCTOBER   ☐ NOVEMBER   ☑ DECEMBER

WHERE DID YOU BUY THE BEANO ANNUAL?

☐ SUPERMARKET
☐ BOOK SHOP
☐ HIGH STREET STORE
☐ LOCAL NEWSAGENT
☐ DIRECT FROM DC THOMSON
☐ ONLINE
OTHER (PLEASE TELL US)........: *From Santa*

WHAT MADE YOU BUY THE BEANO ANNUAL?
(PLEASE TICK ALL ANSWERS THAT APPLY)

☐ I READ THE BEANO COMIC
☐ I BUY THE BEANO COMIC
☐ I SUBSCRIBE TO THE BEANO COMIC
☐ I WATCH DENNIS AND GNASHER ON TV
☐ I HAVE BEANO MERCHANDISE (E.G. TOYS/CLOTHING)
☐ I HAVE VISITED THE BEANO WEBSITE
☐ I HAVE DOWNLOADED THE BEANO DIGITAL EDITION
☐ THE BEANO CHARACTERS
☐ I WAS ATTRACTED BY THE BEANO COVER
☐ THE PRICE
☐ I SAW IT ADVERTISED IN A MAGAZINE/NEWSPAPER/WEBSITE
☐ I'VE BOUGHT THE BEANO ANNUAL BEFORE
☐ I SAW IT ADVERTISED IN A BROCHURE I RECEIVED FROM DC THOMSON
☐ I BUY THE BEANO ANNUAL EVERY YEAR
☐ I WANTED TO KEEP UP/ESTABLISH A FAMILY TRADITION
☐ THERE WAS A PRICE PROMOTION
☐ I WANTED TO INTRODUCE SOMEONE TO THE BEANO

OTHER (PLEASE TELL US)..

DID YOU BUY THE BEANO ANNUAL AS A GIFT FOR SOMEONE?

☑ YES   ☐ NO

IF YES, WAS THE GIFT FOR...

☐ AN ADULT   ☑ A CHILD

AND WAS THAT PERSON...

☐ A SON OR DAUGHTER
☐ A GRANDCHILD
☐ A SIBLING
☐ ANOTHER CHILD
☐ A FRIEND
☐ A SPOUSE OR PARTNER
☐ A PARENT
☐ A GRANDPARENT
OTHER (PLEASE TELL US)..

HAVE YOU BOUGHT THE BEANO ANNUAL BEFORE?

☐ YES   ☑ NO

IF YES, FOR HOW LONG HAVE YOU BEEN BUYING THE BEANO ANNUAL?

☑ 1-2 YEARS   ☐ 3-5 YEARS
☐ 6-10 YEARS   ☐ 10 YEARS +

HAVE YOU EVER BOUGHT ANY OTHER ANNUALS THIS YEAR?

☐ YES   ☑ NO

IF SO, PLEASE TELL US WHICH ONES..
....

HAVE YOU BOUGHT MORE OR LESS ANNUALS THIS YEAR?

☐ MORE   ☐ THE SAME   ☑ LESS

CAN YOU SAY WHY?..
....

B PLEASE ONLY ANSWER THE FOLLOWING QUESTIONS IF YOU ARE THE MAIN READER OF THIS ANNUAL

ARE YOU THE MAIN READER OF THE BEANO ANNUAL?

☑ YES   ☐ NO (PLEASE PROCEED TO SECTION C)

HAVE YOU READ/RECEIVED THIS ANNUAL BEFORE?

☐ YES   ☑ NO

HOW LONG HAVE YOU BEEN READING THE BEANO ANNUAL FOR?

☑ 1-2 YEARS   ☐ 3-5 YEARS
☐ 6-10 YEARS   ☐ 10 YEARS +

THINKING ABOUT THE BEANO ANNUAL AND CHARACTERS, WHICH OF THE FOLLOWING APPLY?
(PLEASE TICK ALL ANSWERS THAT APPLY)

☑ I READ THE BEANO COMIC
☐ I BUY THE BEANO COMIC
☐ I SUBSCRIBE TO THE BEANO COMIC
☐ I WATCH DENNIS & GNASHER ON TV
☐ I HAVE BEANO MERCHANDISE (E.G TOYS/CLOTHING)
☑ I HAVE VISITED THE BEANO WEBSITE
☐ I HAVE DOWNLOADED THE BEANO DIGITAL EDITION

HAVE YOU READ/RECEIVED ANY OTHER ANNUALS THIS YEAR?

☐ YES   ☑ NO

IF SO, PLEASE TELL US WHICH ONES..
....

HAVE YOU READ A DIGITAL EDITION OF AN ANNUAL?

☐ YES
☐ NO BUT I WOULD CONSIDER IT
☑ NO AND I WOULD NOT CONSIDER IT

IF YES, PLEASE TELL US WHICH DIGITAL EDITION ANNUALS YOU HAVE READ
....

C ABOUT YOU

THINKING ABOUT TECHNOLOGY, WHICH OF THE FOLLOWING DEVICES DO YOU OWN?

☐ iPHONE   ☐ SMARTPHONE (EXCLUDING iPHONE)
☐ iPAD   ☐ TABLET PC (EXCLUDING iPAD)
☐ KINDLE   ☐ E-READER (EXCLUDING KINDLE)

ARE YOU?

☐ MALE   ☑ FEMALE

PLEASE TELL US YOUR AGE...

☑ UNDER 7   ☑ 7-10   ☐ 11-14   ☐ 15-19
☐ 20-24   ☐ 25-34   ☐ 35-44   ☐ 45-54
☐ 55-64   ☐ 65-74   ☐ 75+

WHERE DO YOU LIVE?

☐ SE ENGLAND   ☐ SW ENGLAND   ☐ LONDON
☐ EAST OF ENGLAND   ☐ EAST MIDLANDS   ☐ WEST MIDLANDS
☑ YORKS & HUMB   ☐ NE ENGLAND   ☐ NW ENGLAND
☑ SCOTLAND   ☐ WALES   ☐ N IRELAND
☐ EIRE
☐ OVERSEAS (IF SO, PLEASE TELL US WHERE)

....

IF YOU LIVE IN THE UK, PLEASE TELL US YOUR POSTCODE

IV4 8RG

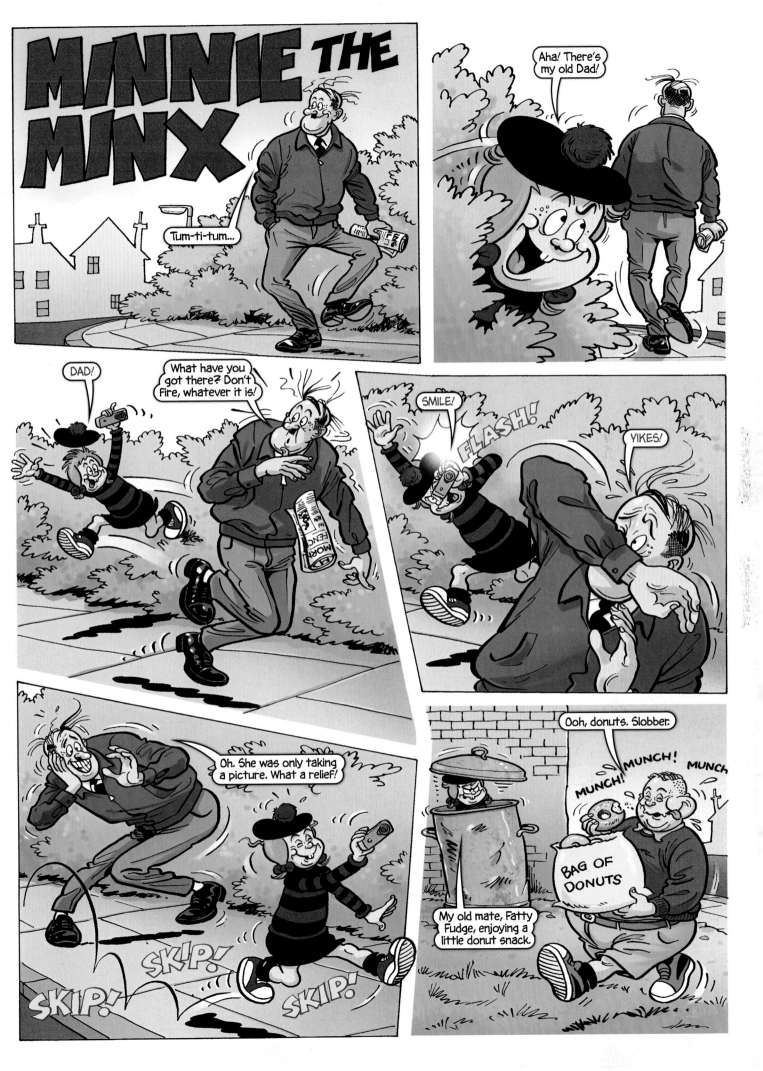

STINKING RICH
A FOUL FABLE

ONCE UPON A TIME, A CUTE LITTLE BABY NAMED RICHARD WAS BORN.

Goo-goo!

HIS MUM WAS SO PROUD - AND ALL THE NURSES SAID HE WAS A BEAUTIFUL BABY.

What a beautiful baby.

SEE? TOLD YOU.

BUT NOT EVERYTHING WAS HOW IT SEEMED WITH THIS LITTLE BABY...

Gnnn...

...BECAUSE HE HAD A SQUEAKY TUMMY.

FFFRRRPPPP

AND HE WASN'T HALF PONGY.

AND HIS PONGY HABITS CARRIED ON THROUGH HIS LIFE. AT NURSERY...

...THINGS WERE NO BETTER.

AT SCHOOL, HE COULDN'T STOP - AND PEOPLE WERE STARTING TO NOTICE.

Oxygen! Need oxygen!

AND WHEN IT CAME TIME TO ASK A GIRL OUT ON A DATE...

...HE DIDN'T HAVE ANY SUCCESS THERE. EVEN THE RHUBARB WILTED FROM HIS TROUSER TRUMPS.

BUT A TV TALENT SCOUT SPOTTED OUR PAL, RICH...

Wanna be a star?

Not interested.

For THIS much?

I'm interested!

SOON HE WAS ON A TALENT SHOW...

BUT HE GOT NERVOUS...

Lots of people watching...

VERY NERVOUS...

Oh, crumbs. I'm going to...

AND SO HIS TV CAREER ENDED BEFORE IT EVEN STARTED.

KARFFOOM

BUT HE WASN'T TOO BOTHERED - BECAUSE HE GOT A HAPPY ENDING...

...MAKING A FORTUNE AS A DEMOLITION EXPERT.

Just call me STINKING RICH!

FFRROOOMM...

VILE TIMES WITH EVIL EDGAR

Potion in the Ocean!

By Philip Minion

1 **A**S a low-level minion in the employ of Doctor E. L. Pumpshoffen, otherwise known as Evil Edgar, I was used to working in the cramped conditions of his underground laboratory.

However, as I swept the path which ran through the forest of fungus two miles below street level, I had a sudden urge to breathe clean, fresh air again.

3 This glance proved to be my undoing, as I tripped on the next step. The next thing I knew, Edgar was speaking as he grabbed my shoulder in one of his claw-like hands. "What an eager volunteer! You've made my minion crew complete!" he said.

STAND BY YOUR KIPPER!

NEMATODE

5 The baboons put on a spurt and pedalled furiously, driving our evil master's U-boat around a U-bend and popping us out into the Atlantic a couple of hundred metres below the surface! The Nematode was a swift vessel and we made steady progress towards the West (I shuddered to think of the horrible nature of the experiments which had led Edgar to discover that the baboons pedalled faster whenever Country and Western music was played over the speaker system).

2 The air in Evil Edgar's lair was fetid and smelled vaguely of baboons, talc and kippers – I could only guess at the vile experiments this maddest of mad scientists was carrying out! Suddenly, I could take it no more and made a dash for the surface, my footsteps ringing on the ancient wrought-iron staircase as I raced upwards. Passing the open door of the next level, I spotted Edgar in a nautical (but nice) outfit, addressing some other minions.

4 Minutes later I found myself climbing aboard Edgar's secret submarine The Nematode in its subterranean mooring. The Nematode was filled with baboon galley slaves on converted pedaloes and my job was to supply them with talc, to prevent chafing, while the other minions fed them kippers to keep their energy levels up.

COUNTRY AND WESTERN MUSIC

WHIRR!

PEDAL!

SPIN

PEDAL FURIOUSLY!

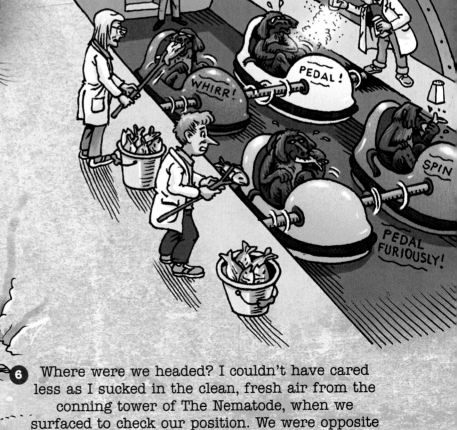

6 Where were we headed? I couldn't have cared less as I sucked in the clean, fresh air from the conning tower of The Nematode, when we surfaced to check our position. We were opposite a deserted cove and Edgar ordered that his personal dinghy be inflated.

NEMATODE

7 That task fell to me and with the combination of a sigh of relief that the C&W music was switched off and the fresh air in my lungs, I swiftly had the dinghy in the water. Edgar's eyes were glowing bright and he looked especially evil as I rowed the dinghy toward the beach, accompanied by Clive, another minion, clutching a brightly-coloured test tube.

9 I shuddered at the horror of this revelation - giving creatures with a reputation for suction a taste for blood-sucking was fiendish indeed!
Edgar turned angrily towards Clive. "The potion isn't working! The limpets remain limp and lifeless – why are they not bloodthirsty?" he demanded.
As Clive struggled for an answer, the water in the rock pool bubbled and frothed before erupting in a fine spume as an enormous crab burst forth.

10 "Far from causing vampirism in limpets the potion's causing gigantism in crustaceans!" exclaimed Clive.
When Edgar saw what was behind him, he took off like a geriatric whippet across the sand, leapt into the dinghy and rowed back to The Nematode, leaving me and Clive to face the claws of the crab alone!

TOSS!

RRIP!

SQUAS

8 We alighted on the sand and Edgar grabbed the tube from Clive, before skipping across the beach towards a small rock pool. He looked for all the world like an excited schoolboy – albeit one with the facial features of a demented ferret. I asked Clive what was in the test tube, as Edgar poured its contents into the rock pool, and he turned pale. "Nobody in 'potions' is quite sure of what it will do outside of laboratory conditions," began Clive, nervously, "but Edgar is hoping it will cause vampirism in limpets! Oh, and it's a nice colour!"

POUR!

11 Fortunately, crab eyesight is poor and it scuttled sideways after the movement of Edgar, grabbing his submarine in one giant claw and using the other as a tin opener.

CREAM TEAS

12 What happened next? Did the killer crustacean end the vile career of Evil Edgar? Who knows? Me and Clive popped up the coast for a cream tea and never looked back!

THE END

DS

The BASH STREET KIDS

Let's have a game of football!

Super idea! My team against your team!

SLAP!

Excuse me, Danny...

TAP!

...Kevin would like a game.

Huh?

Kevin's only a pebble - how good could he be?

SHRUG!

0-0 AT HALF TIME -

Time for the half time oranges!

I need a little more than that!

You're not kidding!

SQUEEZE!

CHOMP! GUZZLE!

ICE CREAM

SUCK!

Spotty's got great dribbling skills!

SPIN!

TWIST!

Ha-ha! He's even tied HIMSELF in knots!

TRIP!

ZONK!

IT'S STILL 0-0 IN THE FINAL MINUTE -

I'm right through on goal!

SPIN!

SPIN!

Penalty!

CRUMP!

Are you blind, ref? That was a good tackle!

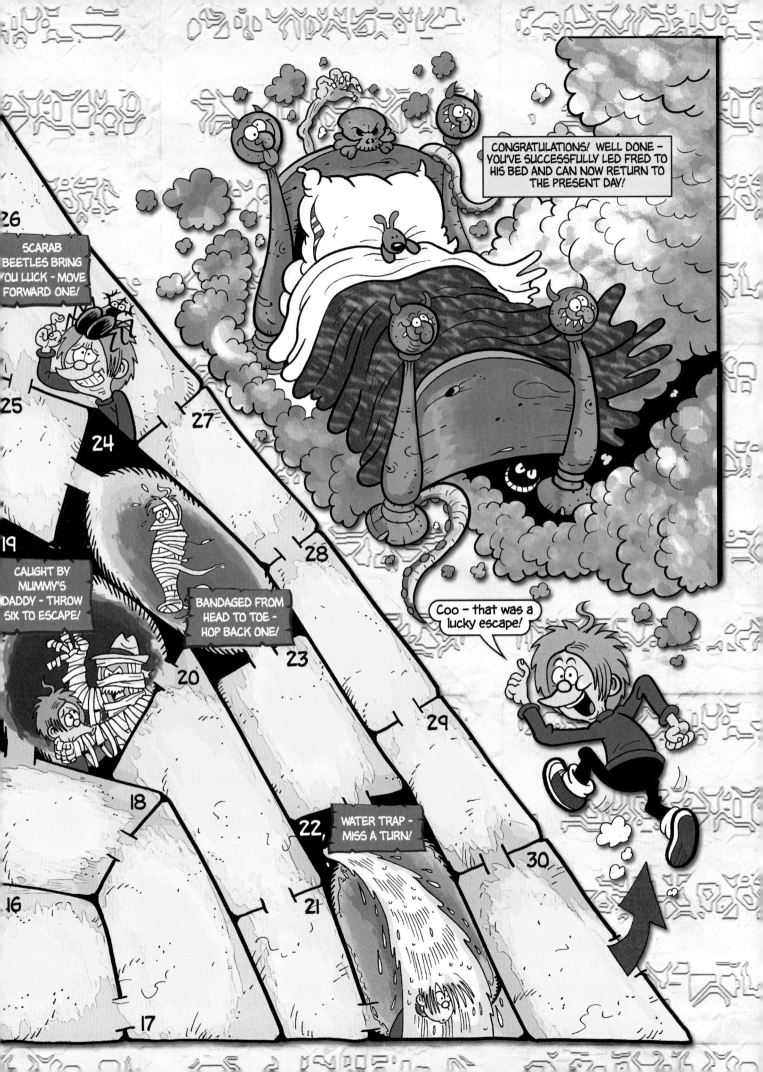

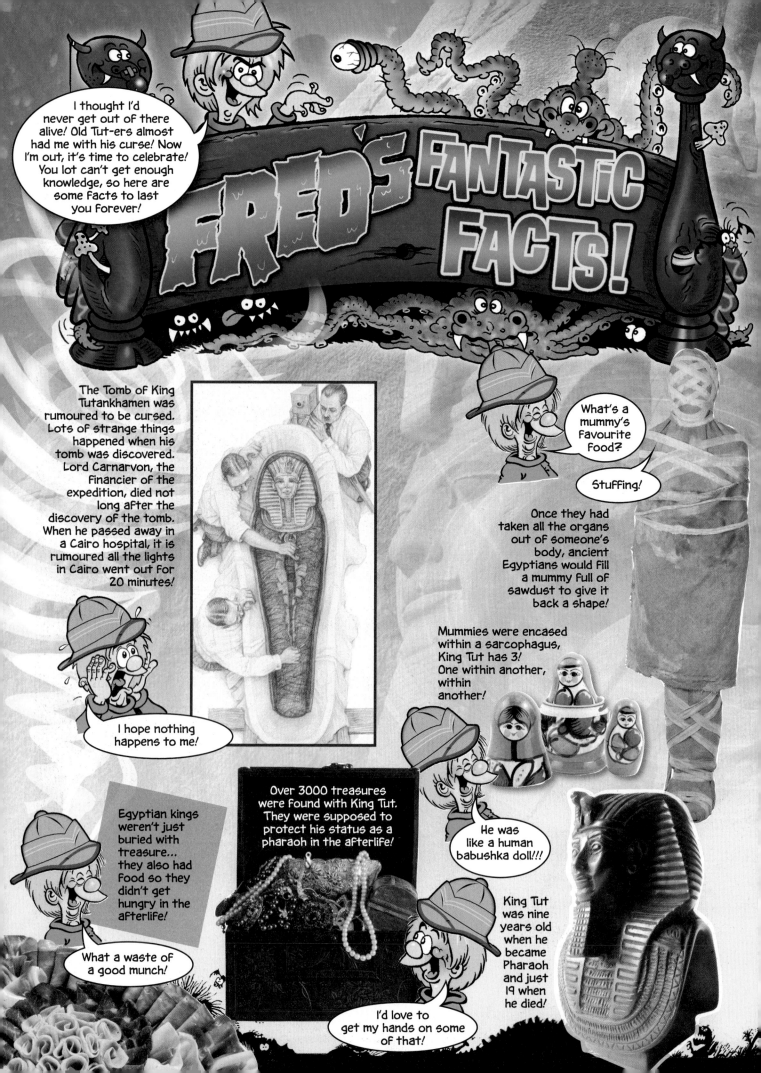

FRED'S FANTASTIC FACTS!

I thought I'd never get out of there alive! Old Tut-ers almost had me with his curse! Now I'm out, it's time to celebrate! You lot can't get enough knowledge, so here are some facts to last you forever!

The Tomb of King Tutankhamen was rumoured to be cursed. Lots of strange things happened when his tomb was discovered. Lord Carnarvon, the financier of the expedition, died not long after the discovery of the tomb. When he passed away in a Cairo hospital, it is rumoured all the lights in Cairo went out for 20 minutes!

I hope nothing happens to me!

What's a mummy's favourite food?

Stuffing!

Once they had taken all the organs out of someone's body, ancient Egyptians would fill a mummy full of sawdust to give it back a shape!

Mummies were encased within a sarcophagus, King Tut has 3! One within another, within another!

Egyptian kings weren't just buried with treasure... they also had food so they didn't get hungry in the afterlife!

What a waste of a good munch!

Over 3000 treasures were found with King Tut. They were supposed to protect his status as a pharaoh in the afterlife!

He was like a human babushka doll!!!

King Tut was nine years old when he became Pharaoh and just 19 when he died!

I'd love to get my hands on some of that!

Meebo is being forced to walk the plank by the dastardly seadog, Zuky. Spot the 5 difference between these two pictures.

Finish this word search while I get rid of this mangy mutt.

You? Deal with me? Hahahaha. No mouse-muncher will ever beat the mighty Zuky.

KONUNDRUMS

Bah! That rotten, fleabag cat has blown me clean in two. Find the way through my glorious guts to bring my precious pieces back together again. Maybe then I'll have my chance at revenge against that mangy moggy.

H	Y	R	F	S	D	N	B	I
,'	O	I	S	O	L	P	X	E
E	R	E	K	C	R	U	S	H
E	T	H	S	A	M	S	H	B
,'	S	N	E	N	N	N	A	M
F	E	L	I	N	E	S	R	O
^	D	O	Y	O	R	A	K	B
S	E	O	N	N	R	Y	K	K
F	N	R	K	E	S	S	E	Y

SHARK

SMASH

SNEAKY

BOMB

CANNON

CRUSH

DESTROY

EXPLOSION

FELINE

FIRE

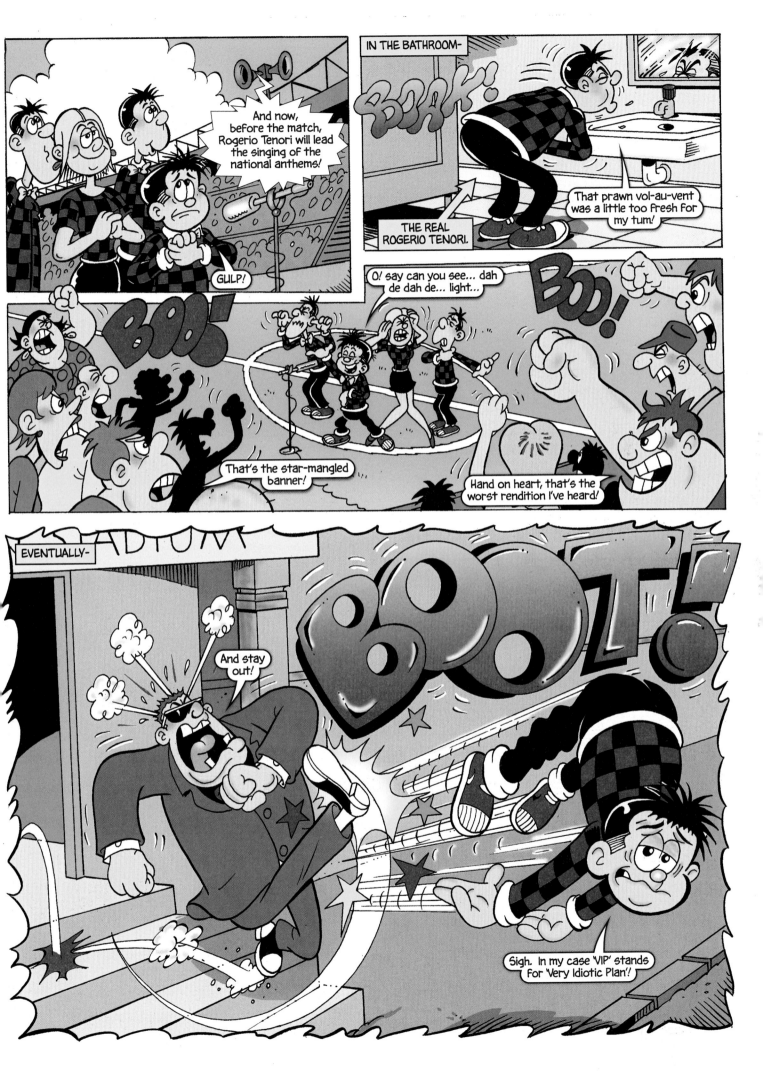

BALL BOY

HE'S FOOTBALL CRAZY!

Were you looking for this, mister?

Mr Ned! What a relief! Thank you!

The game's already kicked off – I just hope I'm not too late!

Oof! Sorry!

GOAL!

My team's already scored. Ho-ho-ho!

Ball Boy – I found Mr Ned! Oh, blast.

He can't hear me over the crowd! This should get his attention...

Sigh! Our luck's not in today.

! GOAL !

Superb header from Mr Ned!

DAVE EASTBURY

BOOT!

Only thirty seconds to go... whoops! My laces have come undone...

TRIP!

Worra stroke of luck.

GOAL!

That must be the winning goal! With the last kick too!

We won the cup! We won the cup!

Championes!

And we've got Mr Ned to thank!

Ah – close enough, I suppose!

CUP WINNERS 2013!

Time for my paper round.

We've got a new delivery for you – here's the address.

Wow!

Better get going.

WHOOSH!

Beanotown flats first!

This lift's always out of order.

Out of order

Dennis and GNASHER®

I am going to make sure Dennis is late for school and gets into trouble.

The detour signs I've made will send him the wrong way.

SCHOOL DETOUR

I suppose we should Follow the detour signs and get to school, Gnasher.

SCHOOL DETOUR

Hee-hee!

This detour is a but messy, Gnasher.

DETOUR

Gnesh!

How many roadworks must they be doing? We're going miles out of our way...

THIS WAY

...miles and MILES! You know, I'm starting to get suspicious about this.

And this is even more suspicious.

You followed the detour? This is for you, then.

PRESS HERE

Hah! I fooled you! You'll never get to school on time. You'll be late and get detention which makes me smarter than you.

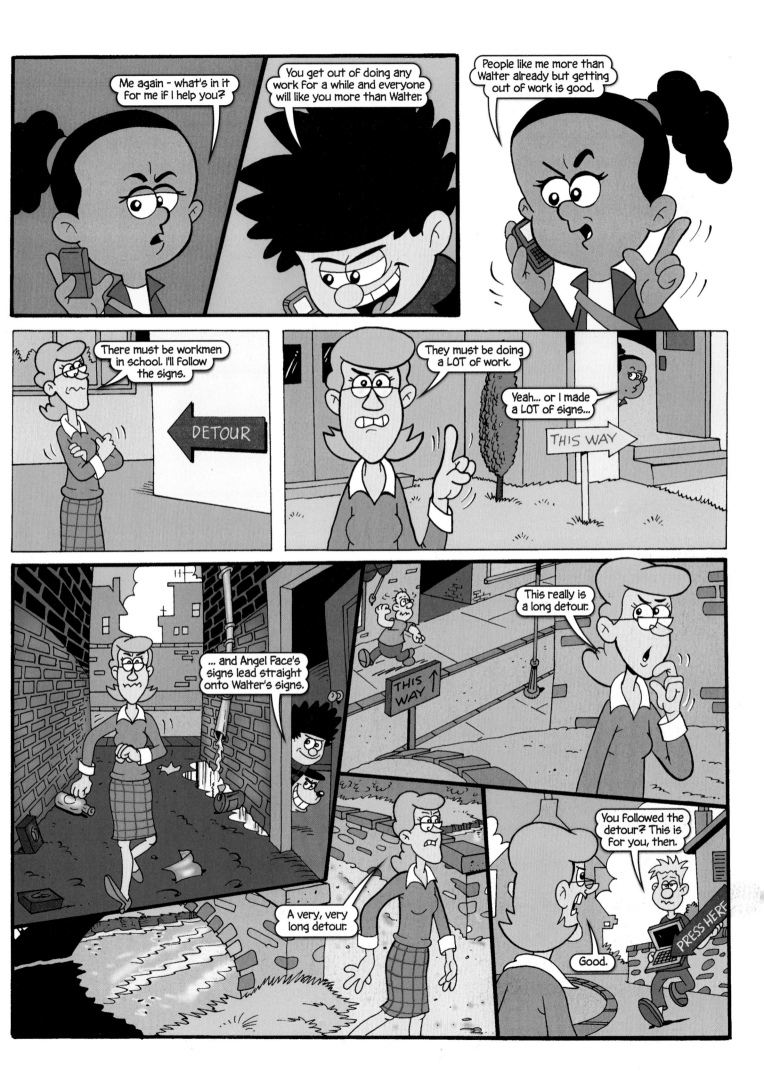